Hyte Y70 Touch User Guide

Customizing Your computer for Performance

Linda B. Jordan

Copyright

All rights reserved. No part of this publication may be reproduced,
distributed, or transmitted in any form or by any means, including
photocopying, recording, or other electronic or mechanical methods,
without the prior written permission of the publisher, except in the case
of brief quotations embodied in critical reviews and certain other
noncommercial uses permitted by copyright law.
Copyright © (Linda B. Jordan), (2024).

Table of Contents

1. Introduction
Overview of the Hyte Y70 Touch
Key Features
What's Included in the Box

2. Getting Started
Unboxing the Hyte Y70 Touch
Case Dimensions and Weight
Required Tools for Assembly

3. Case Design and Features
Exterior Design and Build Quality
14.1-inch 4K Touchscreen Overview
Front, Side, and Top Panels
Vertical GPU Mounting Design
Cable Management Features
Cooling Potential (Radiator and Fan Mounts)

4. Touchscreen Setup
Connecting the Touchscreen
Display Port and Power Connections
Installing the Touchscreen Software
Using the Touchscreen for the First Time
Troubleshooting the Touchscreen Software
Customizing Display Widgets and Features
Using the Screen as a Second Display

5. Component Installation
Installing the Motherboard
Installing the CPU Cooler
Installing Memory Modules
Installing the Graphics Card (Vertical Mount)
Installing Storage Devices (HDD, SSD)
Installing the Power Supply Unit (PSU)
Cable Routing and Management Tips

6. Cooling and Airflow Configuration
Installing Fans (Required Fans Not Included)
Recommended Fan Configurations
Installing Radiators and AIO Coolers
Managing Airflow for Optimal Cooling
Thermal Performance Considerations

7. Software Setup and Configuration
Installing Hyte Nexus Software
Using the Software for Touchscreen Customization
Creating Shortcuts and Widgets
Troubleshooting Software Issues

8. Advanced Customization
Vertical GPU Riser Cable Setup
Adjusting Fan and Radiator Configurations
Installing Additional PCIe Expansion Cards
Optimizing Cable Management for Clean Aesthetics

9. Maintenance and Care
Cleaning the Hyte Y70 Touch Case
Maintaining the Touchscreen

Ensuring Proper Airflow and Dust Management
Checking Internal Temperatures

10. Troubleshooting
Common Installation Issues
Touchscreen Not Working
Software Bugs and Fixes
Resolving Cooling Issues
Accessing the Motherboard with Vertical GPU Installation

11. Specifications
Full Technical Specifications of the Hyte Y70 Touch
Component Compatibility (Motherboard, GPU, PSU, etc.)

12. Warranty and Support
Warranty Information
Contacting Hyte Support
FAQs

13. Conclusion
Final Thoughts on the Hyte Y70 Touch Case
Summary of Key Features and Benefits

Introduction

The Hyte Y70 Touch is a state-of-the-art PC case designed for those who want a unique blend of style, functionality, and cutting-edge technology. Hyte, a company known for pushing the envelope with its designs, took a bold step with the Y70 Touch, offering not only an aesthetic centerpiece but a genuinely functional case for high-performance builds. This is not just any ordinary PC case; it's a visually striking chassis equipped with a 14.1-inch 4K touchscreen that allows for customization and provides additional functionality that is almost unheard of in traditional PC cases.

Standing tall at 47 cm (18.5 inches) and with a width of 32 cm (12.6 inches), the Y70 Touch has a large footprint designed to accommodate the most demanding hardware configurations. Whether you're using an air-cooled or liquid-cooled setup, this case offers ample space for large GPUs, including GPUs like the RTX 4090, and high-performance CPUs. Its dual-chamber layout further enhances airflow by organizing components into separate sections, giving users an easy way to manage cables and optimize cooling.

At its core, the Y70 Touch's most distinguishing feature is its integrated 4K touchscreen, which brings a new level of interactivity and customization to the PC case. Whether you want to monitor system health, display dynamic widgets, or even run a media player or chat window for gaming, this screen offers an entirely new dimension of use that is far more than a simple aesthetic upgrade.

With a hefty price tag reflecting its premium features, the Y70 Touch is aimed at enthusiasts and PC builders who appreciate fine details and are willing to invest in the latest tech. Despite its high cost, this case's incredible build quality and innovation make it an enticing choice for those who want a visually appealing and high-performance system that turns heads while maintaining functionality.

Key Features:

The Hyte Y70 Touch offers a host of advanced features that make it stand out in the crowded world of PC cases. These include the following:

14.1-inch 4K Touchscreen:

The centerpiece of the Y70 Touch, this stunning screen has a resolution of 1100 x 3840 pixels and delivers sharp, vibrant visuals. It can display customizable widgets or even act as a secondary display, adding a unique touch to your system. You can use the touchscreen to monitor hardware stats, control media, view system performance, or integrate with third-party software. The possibilities are endless, and its integration with

Hyte's software suite means that users can customize and fine-tune the display's functionality.

Dual-Chamber Design:

The Y70 Touch's dual-chamber design is both practical and aesthetically pleasing. The case is divided into two sections one for the motherboard, GPU, and cooling system, and the other for the PSU and cables. This layout not only enhances airflow but also helps with cable management, reducing clutter and improving overall airflow. The separate PSU compartment ensures that cables and power-related components do not interfere with the main hardware, allowing for a cleaner and more organized build.

Support for Large Components:

With its spacious interior, the Y70 Touch can easily accommodate high-end components. It supports large GPUs, up to 422mm in length, and can handle massive coolers with a CPU cooler clearance of 180mm. Additionally, the case supports multiple radiator mounts, including up to 360mm options on the roof or side. This makes the case ideal for enthusiasts looking to build a custom liquid-cooled system or those who need to house powerful, space-demanding components.

PCIe Riser Cable Included:

For those who want to display their graphics card vertically, the Y70 Touch includes a high-quality PCIe riser cable. This allows users to mount their GPU in a vertical orientation, showcasing their hardware through the case's stunning glass panels. It's a feature typically found in premium cases and adds to the Y70 Touch's sleek, modern design.

Customizable Cooling Options:

The case does not come with pre-installed fans, giving users the flexibility to choose the best cooling solution for their needs. The Y70 Touch supports up to three 120mm or two 140mm fans on the side, roof, and base, along with a rear fan mount. This open-ended approach gives users the freedom to decide how they want to configure their cooling, whether opting for air cooling or installing a custom AIO liquid cooler.

Tool-less Design:

For ease of assembly and maintenance, the Y70 Touch features a tool-less design. The side and roof panels can be removed and reattached without requiring any tools, making it quick and simple to access the interior for hardware installation or cleaning. This feature makes the case user-friendly, even for those new to PC building.

Premium Build Quality:

The Y70 Touch's construction is solid and well-crafted, with tempered glass side panels and a sturdy steel frame. The case feels robust and secure, with all components fitting together with ease. The large glass panels not only provide a panoramic view of your hardware but also give the case a sleek, modern appearance. The design is available in black, white, and a black/red combo, allowing users to choose the aesthetic that best fits their setup.

What's Included in the Box:

When you purchase the Hyte Y70 Touch, you'll find the following components inside the box:

Hyte Y70 Touch Case:

The case itself, including the front, side, and rear panels, is ready to be configured and customized.

PCIe Riser Cable:

A high-quality PCIe riser cable for vertical GPU mounting, giving users the option to display their GPU through the case's side panels.

Touchscreen:

A 14.1-inch 4K touchscreen that can be mounted in place once the case is assembled. It comes with the necessary cables to connect it to your motherboard and graphics card.

Cable Management Tools:

The case includes several Velcro cable ties to help organize and route cables neatly inside the case. This ensures that even with large hardware configurations, the build remains tidy and airflow is not obstructed.

Instruction Manual:

A detailed guide to help you with the case setup, including installation instructions for the touchscreen and general assembly tips.

Screws and Mounting Hardware:

A set of screws and mounting brackets for installing the motherboard, GPU, PSU, and other components into the case.

USB Cable:

A USB 2.0 cable to connect the touchscreen to your motherboard, enabling its touch functionality.

SATA Power Cable:

A SATA power cable that connects the touchscreen to your power supply for power delivery.

With all these components, the Y70 Touch provides everything you need to get started with building your custom PC, although fans and additional cooling solutions will need to be purchased separately.

This introduction provides a comprehensive overview of the Hyte Y70 Touch, its key features, and what you can expect to find in the box. It lays the groundwork for a deeper dive into the setup, installation, and customization of this innovative case, setting the stage for a premium PC building experience.

Chapter 1.

Getting Started

The experience of unboxing the Hyte Y70 Touch is one of excitement and anticipation, as the case itself is a premium product that promises to elevate any PC build. The packaging is designed to ensure that the case arrives safely, and it's clear that Hyte took extra care to provide a smooth and secure unboxing experience. The case is well-protected by custom foam inserts, which cushion it during transit and prevent any potential damage. These inserts are strategically placed to protect the tempered glass panels, the 14.1-inch touchscreen, and other delicate components.

Upon removing the outer box, you'll be greeted with the sleek, modern look of the Hyte Y70 Touch case. The first thing you'll notice is its bold design, with clean lines, premium glass panels, and a matte finish that conveys both style and durability. As you lift the case out of the box, it feels substantial, underscoring its high-quality construction.

The touchscreen panel is carefully packed to avoid any damage during shipping. It's typically found within its own foam compartment to ensure that it stays protected. Additionally, the box will include a small package of accessories, including the PCIe riser cable, screws, mounting brackets, and a user manual. All of these are neatly arranged to keep everything organized and prevent any small components from being misplaced.

Unboxing the Hyte Y70 Touch is not just about revealing a computer case it's the start of a journey into building your dream PC. The case's elegant presentation and the attention to detail during packaging set the tone for what's to come. Whether you're a seasoned enthusiast or a first-time builder, the unboxing experience reflects the premium nature of the product, ensuring that you start your project on the right note.

Case Dimensions and Weight:

The Hyte Y70 Touch is a large case, and its dimensions reflect the need for ample space to accommodate high-end components and a sizable cooling setup. The case has the following measurements:

Height:

47 cm (18.5 inches)

Width:

32 cm (12.6 inches)

Depth:

43 cm (16.9 inches)

This size makes it a full-sized tower that can comfortably house the largest GPUs, motherboards, and liquid cooling solutions. It's an excellent choice for those looking to build a top-tier PC with room for expansion or customization.

The spacious interior is designed to support both air and custom liquid cooling solutions. The case's internal layout, with its dual-chamber design, allows for easy access to hardware installation and efficient airflow management. You'll have enough room for GPUs up to 422 mm in length, which is crucial for those who plan on using the latest and most powerful graphics cards, like the RTX 4090.

In terms of weight, the Hyte Y70 Touch comes in at approximately 12.7 kg (28 lbs). This is relatively heavy for a case, especially considering it lacks pre-installed fans. The weight is due to the high-quality materials used in its construction, including tempered glass panels and a reinforced steel frame. The weight also speaks to the robustness and durability of the case this is a case built to last, capable of supporting heavy components and standing the test of time.

The size and weight of the Y70 Touch may be a consideration for users with limited space on their desks or those who need to transport their system frequently. However, the weight also contributes to its stability, ensuring that the case remains firmly in place and does not easily tip over during use or installation.

Required Tools for Assembly:

One of the standout features of the Hyte Y70 Touch is its tool-less design, which allows for easy access to the case's interior and simplifies assembly. However, while most parts can be installed without tools, you will still need a few basic tools to complete the assembly process and ensure that everything is properly installed and secure. Here's a list of the tools and accessories you will need:

Screwdriver:

A standard Phillips-head screwdriver is the main tool you'll need for assembling the Y70 Touch. While the case is largely tool-less, you'll still need the screwdriver to secure components like the motherboard, power supply, and any additional hardware like storage devices or add-on cards. It's recommended to use a magnetic screwdriver to help with ease of handling small screws, especially when working inside the case.

Cable Management Tools:

While the Y70 Touch comes with some cable ties, you may want to have additional cable management tools, such as Velcro cable ties or cable clips, on hand to ensure your wiring is neatly organized and doesn't obstruct airflow. This is particularly important if you are using large GPUs, custom cooling systems, or have a complex cable setup.

Anti-static Wrist Strap:

While not strictly required, an anti-static wrist strap is a good precaution to prevent electrostatic discharge (ESD) when handling sensitive components like your motherboard, CPU, or RAM. This is especially important if you plan to install high-end components or are working in an environment where static electricity might be a concern.

Thermal Paste (if installing a CPU cooler):

If you're installing a CPU cooler, you'll need thermal paste to ensure proper heat transfer between your CPU and the cooler. Many coolers come with pre-applied thermal paste, but if you're using a custom cooler or prefer a high-quality paste, this is something to keep in mind.

Screws and Mounting Brackets:

Fortunately, the Y70 Touch includes all the necessary screws and mounting brackets for securing your motherboard, PSU, GPU, and storage devices. However, it's always a good idea to check your components beforehand to make sure that the screws included with the case are compatible with your specific hardware.

Fans or Cooling Solutions:

If you plan to install fans or liquid cooling, you'll need additional screws to mount these components in place. The case doesn't come with fans by default, so it's essential to purchase fans or an AIO liquid cooler separately and have the necessary mounting hardware ready.

Although the Hyte Y70 Touch is a premium, easy-to-assemble case, being prepared with the right tools will help ensure that the building process goes smoothly and that your system is secure, well-ventilated, and operating optimally.

Assembly Tips:

1. Start with the PSU:

Before you begin installing components, it's often a good idea to start with the PSU (power supply) and mount it in the dedicated PSU compartment. This will give you a clearer idea of how to route cables effectively later on.

2. Use Cable Management Features:

Take full advantage of the cable management features built into the case. The dual-chamber design offers plenty of room for routing cables, and the case comes with Velcro cable ties to keep your cables tidy. A clean, organized build not only looks better but also helps improve airflow and system performance.

3. Test Fit Components:

Given the spacious interior of the Y70 Touch, you have the flexibility to test fit your components before securing them permanently. This ensures everything fits well, particularly when dealing with large GPUs and liquid cooling solutions.

In this section, we've explored how to get started with the Hyte Y70 Touch, from unboxing the case to understanding its dimensions, weight, and the tools you'll need for assembly. With this knowledge, you're well on your way to building a customized, high-performance PC using one of the most innovative cases available today.

Chapter 2.

Case Design and Features

The Hyte Y70 Touch is a case that combines cutting-edge design with top-tier functionality. Every aspect of the case is purposefully crafted to provide the best user experience, not only in terms of aesthetics but also with the capability to house powerful hardware and complex cooling systems. This section will take you through the design and features of the Y70 Touch, focusing on the exterior build quality, the 14.1-inch touchscreen, and its innovative design elements, such as vertical GPU mounting and cable management systems.

Exterior Design and Build Quality:

The exterior of the Hyte Y70 Touch is a masterclass in modern PC case design. The case adopts a sleek, minimalistic aesthetic, with clean lines, a matte black finish, and large tempered glass panels. The overall design exudes premium quality, which is evident in both the materials and construction. The frame is made from high-quality steel, which ensures durability while remaining relatively lightweight compared to other full-sized tower cases. The tempered glass panels on the front, side, and top offer a clear view of the internals, providing an excellent platform for showing off high-end components, custom lighting, and liquid cooling solutions.

The build quality of the Y70 Touch is exceptional. The frame is sturdy and provides a solid foundation for even the heaviest components. The glass panels are thick and strong, offering protection while showcasing the system inside. The case feels robust yet is surprisingly easy to handle. Thanks to its well-engineered structure, there's no flex or warping, even during assembly. All edges are smoothed and finished with care, ensuring a premium feel. The front and side panels attach firmly to the chassis, and the mechanism that holds them in place feels secure, meaning there's no risk of accidental detachment.

This quality extends to the overall weight of the case while heavier than some, the weight adds to its stability and reinforces its premium construction. The exterior design is not only aesthetically pleasing but also built to last, capable of withstanding the wear and tear of regular usage while maintaining a sharp look.

14.1-inch 4K Touchscreen Overview:

The star feature of the Hyte Y70 Touch is undoubtedly its 14.1-inch 4K touchscreen that resides at the front of the case. This screen represents a bold move in case design, offering unparalleled customization options and functionality. The screen has a resolution of 1100 x 3840 pixels, offering crisp visuals that make it a perfect addition for users who want a multifunctional display on their PC case.

The touchscreen can be used in a variety of ways. Hyte's proprietary software allows you to integrate several functionalities, such as displaying Twitch chat, monitoring system performance (such as temperature, fan speed, and CPU/GPU usage), or setting up shortcuts for quick access to essential applications. Users can customize the screen layout to suit their needs, making it a unique addition for gamers, streamers, and content creators. The potential for customization is vast, allowing you to make the most of your body's capabilities.

The touchscreen is responsive and fluid, offering a smooth user interface that is easy to navigate. While the software is still in beta, Hyte has shown its commitment to improving and expanding the functionality of the touchscreen. As more features are added, the possibilities for what you can do with this screen will continue to grow, making it a valuable addition to any system.

Front, Side, and Top Panels:

The front panel of the Hyte Y70 Touch is entirely covered with tempered glass, providing a clear view of the internals. The glass is treated to be fingerprint-resistant, maintaining a clean look even after prolonged use. It serves as both an aesthetic feature and a practical one, offering a window into the components inside. This is particularly beneficial for those who want to showcase custom cooling loops, RGB lighting, or unique hardware choices.

The side panel mirrors the front panel's sleek, minimalist design, providing an unobstructed view of the interior. The tempered glass on the side is designed to offer a clear, full view of the interior components. It's also attached via a simple latch mechanism, making it easy to remove and reattach when necessary. The side panel, like the rest of the case, is sturdy and well-secured, ensuring that once it's in place, it will stay firmly attached.

The top panel is where the case stands out in terms of both function and form. It's made from a combination of steel and tempered glass, with plenty of ventilation for airflow. The top panel is designed to be modular and provides mounting points for additional fans or radiators. Additionally, it features an integrated mesh filter to help with airflow, ensuring that dust doesn't easily enter the system through the top.

Vertical GPU Mounting Design:

One of the most distinctive features of the Hyte Y70 Touch is its vertical GPU mounting design. Unlike traditional horizontal mounting, which can sometimes block the view of high-end graphics cards, the Y70 Touch positions the GPU vertically, allowing for a clear and unobstructed view of the entire card. This setup not only enhances the visual appeal of the system but also allows users to showcase their GPUs, especially those with striking designs or custom cooling setups.

Vertical mounting provides ample space for larger graphics cards, making it ideal for high-end GPUs like the RTX 4090, which can be bulky and require more room than traditional designs offer. This feature ensures that users don't have to compromise on GPU size when choosing components for their build.

However, it's worth noting that to use the vertical GPU mount, the Hyte Y70 Touch includes a PCIe riser cable, which facilitates the connection between the GPU and the motherboard. This riser cable is custom-designed to fit the case, ensuring that the GPU is mounted securely and has the necessary connections for power and data transmission. The vertical GPU mount is one of the standout features that adds both functionality and visual appeal to the build.

Cable Management Features:

The Hyte Y70 Touch includes a well-thought-out cable management system, designed to keep cables organized and out of sight. It features multiple cable routing channels and tie-down points, allowing you to route cables neatly behind the motherboard tray. This ensures that cables don't obstruct airflow, maintaining optimal cooling performance.

The cable management bar at the top of the case provides additional support for organizing cables, particularly those from the power supply and fans. This bar, along with the built-in Velcro straps, gives users the ability to bundle cables and secure them tightly, reducing clutter inside the case. Moreover, the design allows for a clean, cable-free aesthetic when looking through the tempered glass panels.

For users who plan to install custom water cooling systems or large GPUs, the cable management system is robust enough to handle the additional wiring that comes with these components. With careful planning, you can ensure that your build looks as clean and professional on the inside as it does on the outside.

Cooling Potential (Radiator and Fan Mounts):

The Hyte Y70 Touch excels in cooling potential. The case is designed to accommodate a wide range of cooling options, including both air and liquid cooling solutions. The case supports multiple radiator mounts, with positions available in the front, top, and bottom of the case. This provides plenty of flexibility for users to install powerful custom water-cooling loops or high-performance AIO liquid coolers.

The front of the case can support up to a 360mm radiator, while the top can accommodate a 240mm or 280mm radiator. The bottom also has space for a 120mm radiator, allowing users to install a combination of fans and radiators to achieve optimal cooling performance. With these options, users can build a system that stays cool under load, even with high-end components like the latest GPUs and CPUs.

Additionally, the case has ample space for mounting fans. It supports up to three 120mm or two 140mm fans in the front, two 120mm or 140mm fans on the top, and one 120mm fan at the bottom. The multiple fan mounts, combined with the large air intakes and exhausts, ensure that the Hyte Y70 Touch has excellent airflow, keeping components cool even during intense gaming sessions or resource-heavy tasks.

The Hyte Y70 Touch is a case that balances innovative features with practical design. From its premium build quality to its customizable touchscreen, vertical GPU mounting, and impressive cooling potential, this case offers everything a PC enthusiast could need for their next high-performance build. Whether you're looking to showcase your components, build a custom cooling loop, or enjoy easy cable management, the Y70 Touch delivers on all fronts.

Chapter 3.

Touchscreen Setup

The 14.1-inch 4K touchscreen of the Hyte Y70 Touch is one of the standout features of the case, offering a whole new level of functionality. Setting up and integrating this screen into your system may seem like a complex task, but with the right instructions, it's straightforward. This section will guide you through connecting the touchscreen, installing the necessary software, troubleshooting, and customizing the display to fit your needs. By the end of this guide, you'll have your touchscreen set up and ready to use, enhancing your experience with the Hyte Y70 Touch case.

Connecting the Touchscreen:

The touchscreen is designed to integrate seamlessly with the Hyte Y70 Touch case. To connect the screen, you'll need to ensure that both the DisplayPort and power cables are correctly linked to the motherboard and power supply. The DisplayPort cable is responsible for transmitting the video signal, while the power cable connects to the system's power supply to provide the necessary energy for the touchscreen to operate.

Before beginning, ensure that your PC is powered off to prevent any electrical mishaps during installation. Locate the PCIe slot on the motherboard where the custom PCIe riser card for the touchscreen is intended to be connected. Insert the DisplayPort cable into the riser card's port, ensuring a secure and firm connection. The power cable should be connected to a dedicated power cable from your system's power supply. The cables are designed to reach their respective connectors without tension, so make sure to arrange them neatly to avoid cable strain or damage.

After securing the cables, carefully attach the touchscreen to its designated mount on the front of the case. Once physically connected, you're ready to power up your PC and proceed with software installation.

Display Port and Power Connections:

As previously mentioned, the touchscreen requires both a DisplayPort connection and a power supply connection. These two elements are key to its functionality.

The DisplayPort connection enables the touchscreen to receive the signal from the GPU, which is then displayed on the screen. DisplayPort offers higher resolutions and refresh rates, which makes it an excellent choice for high-quality displays like the Hyte Y70 Touch's 4K touchscreen. The connection is typically located on a custom PCIe riser card, which ensures that the touchscreen is both powered and receives the video signal directly from the GPU, optimizing the display's performance.

In addition to the DisplayPort, the power connection is essential to run the touchscreen. It draws power from your PC's power supply unit (PSU), and its connection is simple usually a standard SATA power cable or a Molex connector, depending on the PSU type and configuration. Once these two connections are made, the touchscreen should automatically power on when the system is booted up.

Make sure that both cables are connected securely before proceeding to software installation. A loose connection can lead to an improper setup or display issues.

Installing the Touchscreen Software:

After physically connecting the touchscreen, the next step is installing the Hyte touchscreen software. The touchscreen comes with a software suite that needs to be installed to enable its full functionality. The software is designed to help you configure the screen, customize widgets, and integrate various features for enhanced interactivity.

To begin, navigate to Hyte's official website and download the touchscreen software. It is typically available in the downloads section under support or drivers for the Hyte Y70 Touch case. Ensure that you download the version specific to your system's operating system, whether you're using Windows or Linux.

Once downloaded, run the installer and follow the on-screen instructions to complete the installation process. The software will guide you through setting up the touchscreen interface, configuring display settings, and checking that the hardware is functioning correctly. During installation, you may be prompted to restart your computer to finalize the process.

After installation, the software should automatically launch, and you'll be able to start interacting with your touchscreen.

Using the Touchscreen for the First Time:

When the touchscreen is successfully connected and the software installed, it's time to use it for the first time. Upon booting up your system, the touchscreen should power on automatically. The software will detect the display and initialize the interface. The first thing you'll see is the default screen layout, which typically includes essential system monitoring widgets like CPU usage, temperature readings, fan speeds, and memory usage.

To start using the touchscreen, simply tap the screen to interact with the software interface. You can navigate through different widgets and settings using touch gestures, such as swiping to change views or tapping to open shortcuts. The touchscreen responds well to touch inputs, making it intuitive to use.

If you encounter any issues where the touchscreen is not responding to input, double-check the connection cables to ensure everything is securely attached. Also, confirm that the Hyte software is running in the background and has detected the touchscreen correctly.

Troubleshooting the Touchscreen Software:

While the Hyte Y70 Touch is designed to work seamlessly, occasional issues with the touchscreen or software may arise. Here are some common troubleshooting steps:

1. Screen Not Responding:

Ensure that the DisplayPort cable is securely connected to both the screen and the GPU. If the screen remains unresponsive, check the power cable connection to the PSU. Try rebooting the system to reset the hardware connections.

2. Touchscreen Flickering or Lagging:

If you experience flickering or lag, this may be due to a software glitch or a compatibility issue with your system. Check for software updates, as newer versions of the touchscreen software may have fixed bugs that cause performance issues.

3. Display Not Detecting:

If the touchscreen is not displaying anything, ensure that the DisplayPort connection is firmly inserted into both the riser card and the GPU. Also, verify that the monitor is set to the correct display mode via the system's display settings.

4. Screen Calibration Issues:

If touch inputs are inaccurate or not aligned with the display, calibrate the touchscreen via the software settings. There is typically an option within the software to calibrate the touch input to ensure that the screen responds correctly to your gestures.

Customizing Display Widgets and Features:

One of the most exciting aspects of the Hyte Y70 Touch is the ability to customize the display and make it work exactly how you want it. The touchscreen software includes a variety of widgets and features that can be placed on the screen. These include:

System Monitoring:

Display real-time metrics such as CPU/GPU temperature, load, fan speed, and memory usage.

Media Controls:

Use the touchscreen as a media control hub for your favorite apps like Spotify, YouTube, or even your video player.

Shortcuts:

Add shortcuts to essential applications or tools, allowing you to launch programs or websites directly from the screen.

Twitch Chat and Alerts:

Streamers can integrate their Twitch chat, follower notifications, or other streaming alerts directly onto the touchscreen.

To customize these widgets, simply open the software interface and drag and drop the widgets into your preferred position. You can resize and reorganize them to suit your workflow. Some software updates may even introduce new widgets or functionality, allowing for even more customization options as the touchscreen software evolves.

Using the Screen as a Second Display:

The Hyte Y70 Touch can also be used as a second display, thanks to its DisplayPort connectivity. Once the software is installed, you can set the touchscreen to function as an additional monitor. This is perfect for multitasking, offering a place to display your web browser, chat windows, or other useful tools without cluttering your main screen.

To use the touchscreen as a second display, simply navigate to your computer's display settings and enable it as an extended monitor. You can configure its resolution, orientation, and display mode (e.g., landscape or portrait) depending on your needs. With its 4K resolution, the touchscreen provides ample space for productivity applications or monitoring tools, making it a valuable asset for power users.

Setting up the Hyte Y70 Touch touchscreen is a straightforward process, and once fully configured, it adds significant functionality to your PC build. Whether you're customizing the display, using it as a second monitor, or troubleshooting any issues, you'll soon be able to take full advantage of this innovative feature, enhancing your PC experience with endless possibilities.

Chapter 4.

Component Installation

Building a custom PC in the Hyte Y70 Touch case is an exciting experience, thanks to its spacious interior and thoughtful design features. This section will guide you through the installation process for each key component in your system. Whether you're a first-time builder or a seasoned veteran, you'll find step-by-step instructions to help you properly install and configure the components. We'll cover everything from the motherboard to cable management, ensuring your build is both functional and visually appealing.

Installing the Motherboard:

The motherboard is the heart of your PC, so installing it correctly is essential for ensuring your system runs smoothly. The Hyte Y70 Touch case is designed to accommodate a variety of motherboard sizes, including ATX, Micro-ATX, and E-ATX form factors, making it versatile for different builds.

Start by aligning the I/O shield (the metal plate that covers the ports on the back of the motherboard) with the rear of the case. Once it's in place, carefully lower the motherboard into the case. The motherboard will line up with the mounting standoffs inside the case. These standoffs are usually pre-installed, but check if they need to be adjusted for the specific motherboard form factor you're using.

Secure the motherboard with screws provided in the case or motherboard package. Ensure the motherboard is seated firmly and is not shifting around. Take extra care to avoid over-tightening the screws, as this can damage the motherboard or cause it to flex, leading to potential issues down the line.

Installing the CPU Cooler:

Once the motherboard is installed, it's time to install the CPU cooler. Depending on the type of cooler you're using (air or liquid), the process will differ slightly.

For air coolers, start by applying a small amount of thermal paste to the top of the CPU. Many air coolers come with thermal paste pre-applied to their base, so check if it's included before applying more. Then, align the cooler with the mounting brackets on the motherboard and gently lower it onto the CPU. Secure the cooler with the screws provided, ensuring it sits evenly and firmly on the CPU.

If you're using a liquid cooler, the process involves mounting the radiator and pump unit. For the Hyte Y70 Touch, the case offers ample room for both front and top radiator mounting, depending on the cooler's size and your preference. Install the radiator in the desired location, ensuring there's enough clearance for fans and other components. Next, mount the pump unit onto the CPU socket, aligning it with the screws or brackets provided.

Regardless of the type of cooler you use, ensure the installation is secure and the cooler is making proper contact with the CPU. This ensures optimal thermal performance.

Installing Memory Modules:

Next, install your RAM (memory) modules. The Hyte Y70 Touch case has plenty of space around the motherboard, which allows for easy access to memory slots.

Open the clips on both sides of each RAM slot, then align the notch on the memory stick with the slot's key. Gently but firmly press down on the module until you hear the clip snap into place. Ensure that the memory modules are seated evenly and securely. If you're installing multiple modules, consult your motherboard's manual to determine the best slots to use for optimal dual-channel or quad-channel performance.

For high-performance memory, consider installing the modules in pairs for better memory bandwidth. Double-check that the modules are fully seated by giving them a gentle push after installation.

Installing the Graphics Card (Vertical Mount):

The Hyte Y70 Touch case features a vertical GPU mount, which is a key design element that enhances the aesthetics of your build. To install your graphics card in this vertical position, you'll need to use the included PCIe riser cable. This cable allows the GPU to be mounted vertically while maintaining the necessary connection to the motherboard.

Begin by removing the necessary PCIe slot covers on the case. These covers are located on the rear panel and can be removed by unscrewing the screws holding them in place. Afterward, align the GPU with the PCIe riser card's connector and carefully insert it into the PCIe slot on the motherboard. Ensure the connector is fully seated.

Once the GPU is inserted, secure it in place by screwing the mounting brackets into the case. The vertical mount design ensures that your GPU is displayed prominently, showcasing its design while maximizing airflow. Make sure the GPU is securely locked into place to avoid any movement or potential damage during use.

Installing Storage Devices (HDD, SSD):

Installing storage devices is a relatively simple process, but it's crucial to properly organize your drives to ensure optimal airflow and easy access. The Hyte Y70 Touch case offers multiple mounting options for both HDDs (Hard Disk Drives) and SSDs (Solid State Drives).

To begin, identify the designated mounting areas for storage. The case typically includes several trays and brackets for mounting both 2.5-inch SSDs and 3.5-inch HDDs. Start by inserting the SSD into the appropriate tray, securing it with screws to hold it in place. For HDDs, the process is similar: slide the drive into the HDD cage, and secure it with screws.

Once the drives are mounted, connect them to the motherboard using the SATA cables. The power cables for the drives will be connected to the PSU. Ensure that the cables are routed neatly to prevent obstruction of airflow.

Installing the Power Supply Unit (PSU):

The PSU powers all your components, so it's essential to install it correctly. The Hyte Y70 Touch case offers a dedicated compartment for the PSU, usually located at the bottom of the case.

Begin by sliding the PSU into its compartment, ensuring the fan faces the bottom of the case (or upwards, depending on your airflow preference). Secure the PSU with screws to keep it firmly in place.

Next, connect the necessary power cables to the motherboard, GPU, and storage devices. The 24-pin ATX cable connects to the motherboard, while the 8-pin CPU cable connects to the CPU power socket. The 6+2 PCIe cables should be connected to the GPU, while the SATA power cables provide power to your SSDs and HDDs.

Ensure that all cables are routed in a way that maintains airflow and doesn't obstruct other components. Neatly tie off excess cables with cable ties to keep everything organized.

Cable Routing and Management Tips:

Proper cable management not only improves the aesthetics of your build but also helps with airflow, cooling, and easy maintenance. The Hyte Y70 Touch case offers several cable management features, such as velcro straps, grommets, and routing channels to help keep cables out of sight.

Start by routing cables behind the motherboard tray, making use of the grommet holes to pass cables through. This will keep cables organized and prevent them from interfering with airflow. For cables that need to be visible or extend across the case, try to bundle them together neatly with cable ties to minimize clutter.

Take your time when routing cables to ensure there's adequate space around airflow areas, especially near fans and radiators. Avoid cramming cables into tight spaces, as this can restrict airflow and increase the temperature of your system.

With proper cable management, your build will not only look clean and professional but will also perform better by ensuring efficient airflow and cooling.

The process of installing components into the Hyte Y70 Touch case is straightforward due to its spacious interior and thoughtful design. By following these steps, you can ensure that your system is installed correctly and performs optimally. With attention to detail during the build process, you'll have a well-organized, aesthetically pleasing, and high-performance PC.

Chapter 5.

Cooling and Airflow Configuration

Proper cooling is essential to maintain the performance and longevity of your components, especially in a high-performance PC build. The Hyte Y70 Touch case, with its spacious interior and flexibility, allows users to configure their cooling solution to meet the demands of even the most powerful hardware. This section will guide you through installing fans and radiators, selecting the best fan configurations, managing airflow, and optimizing thermal performance for a cooler, quieter system.

Installing Fans (Required Fans Not Included):

One important thing to note about the Hyte Y70 Touch case is that it does not come with pre-installed fans. While this allows for customization and ensures you can choose the fans that best suit your cooling needs and aesthetic preferences, it also means you will need to purchase fans separately. The case supports various fan sizes, with 120mm and 140mm fans being the most common.

Before you begin installing your fans, ensure you have the necessary fans for your build. The Y70 Touch supports multiple fan placements, including the front, top, and bottom sections. Fans should be installed with the correct airflow direction in mind to maximize cooling performance. The intake fans should be placed at the front or bottom of the case to pull cool air in, while exhaust fans should be placed at the top or rear to expel hot air out of the system.

Start by determining where you want your intake and exhaust fans. For example, you can install three 120mm intake fans in the front and two 120mm exhaust fans in the top or rear. This configuration offers efficient airflow by bringing cool air in from the front and pushing hot air out from the top or rear. Installing fans at the bottom is also an option if you want to enhance intake airflow further, but it's typically less common.

To install the fans, align the fan's mounting holes with the corresponding holes in the case. Secure the fan with the included screws and ensure the airflow direction is correct. Most fans have an arrow on the frame to indicate airflow direction, so be sure to position them properly to avoid disrupting the case's overall airflow pattern.

Recommended Fan Configurations:

While fan configuration largely depends on the hardware being used and the desired cooling setup, there are several general fan configuration guidelines that can help ensure your system is cooled effectively.

Balanced Airflow:

A balanced airflow configuration aims to have an equal number of intake and exhaust fans. For example, you could install three 120mm intake fans in the front and three 120mm exhaust fans at the top or rear. This provides a constant supply of cool air and helps exhaust the hot air efficiently, preventing hot spots inside the case.

Positive Airflow:

In some cases, users prefer a positive airflow setup, where the intake fans outnumber the exhaust fans. This configuration is often used when you want to ensure that dust is kept out of the case, as more intake airflow helps create a pressure differential that can reduce the amount of dust entering through the case's openings. For example, you could install three 120mm intake fans in the front and two 120mm exhaust fans at the top or rear.

Negative Airflow:

Alternatively, some users choose a negative airflow configuration, where exhaust fans outnumber intake fans. This setup can be useful in scenarios where components such as GPUs or CPUs generate significant heat, as it pulls the heat away from those components more aggressively. However, it can increase the risk of dust buildup if there are not enough intake fans to filter the air effectively. A negative airflow configuration might look like two 120mm intake fans in the front and three 120mm exhaust fans at the top or rear.

The ideal fan configuration depends on your specific hardware, cooling needs, and noise tolerance. It's often a good idea to experiment with different setups to find the one that offers the best thermal performance for your system.

Installing Radiators and AIO Coolers:

For those looking to take their cooling performance a step further, the Hyte Y70 Touch case supports the installation of radiators and All-In-One (AIO) liquid coolers. AIO coolers are an excellent choice for keeping your CPU cool, especially if you're overclocking or using a high-performance processor.

The case offers ample space for both front-mounted and top-mounted radiators. It can support radiators up to 360mm in length at the front and 280mm at the top. Depending on your needs, you can choose between different-sized radiators, with 120mm to 360mm being the most common sizes.

To install an AIO cooler, first mount the radiator in the desired position, either at the front or top of the case. If you're installing a front-mounted radiator, ensure the fans are positioned to push air into the case, while a top-mounted radiator should have the fans set to exhaust air out. Once the radiator is in place, secure the fans to the radiator, then connect the pump unit to the CPU socket following the instructions provided by the cooler's manufacturer.

Make sure that there is adequate clearance for the radiator, especially in the front and top areas. The Hyte Y70 Touch case has enough space to handle even large AIO coolers, but it's always good to check for any obstructions before beginning installation.

Managing Airflow for Optimal Cooling:

Managing airflow is crucial for achieving optimal cooling performance. The Hyte Y70 Touch case is designed to maximize airflow with multiple fan mounts, but it's important to strategically position your cooling components to prevent hot air from circulating within the case.

Start by determining the flow direction of your fans. Intake fans should be placed at the front or bottom, and exhaust fans should be at the top or rear. The primary goal is to create a steady flow of air from the front (cool) to the back (hot) of the case. The airflow should flow smoothly through the case, with minimal obstructions.

Avoid creating areas of stagnant air, where heat can accumulate and cause components to overheat. For instance, placing too many fans in one area can disrupt airflow and create hotspots. Be mindful of your fan positions, and make sure the air flows efficiently through the case.

Thermal Performance Considerations:

When it comes to thermal performance, the Hyte Y70 Touch case is designed to handle demanding hardware. However, your choice of fans, radiators, and cooling configuration can have a significant impact on the overall thermal performance.

A good starting point is to monitor your CPU, GPU, and system temperatures to see how they perform under load. If your system is running too hot, you may need to adjust the number or placement of your fans or consider upgrading to higher-performance fans or a larger radiator.

In addition to fan configurations, make sure your components are properly seated and that there is good contact between your CPU and cooler. Poor thermal paste application or an improperly installed cooler can result in higher temperatures, even with good airflow.

Lastly, consider noise levels when configuring your cooling setup. High-performance fans can generate significant noise, but you can mitigate this by using quieter fans or adjusting fan speeds through software or BIOS settings. Balancing cooling and noise is key to achieving a comfortable and efficient system.

Optimizing cooling and airflow in the Hyte Y70 Touch case is an important step to ensuring your PC remains cool under load, operates quietly, and performs at its best. By carefully selecting and installing fans, radiators, and AIO coolers, and managing airflow for maximum efficiency, you can create a custom PC that excels in both performance and longevity.

Chapter 6.

Software Setup and Configuration

The Hyte Y70 Touch case introduces an exciting and innovative feature: a 14.1-inch 4K touchscreen that can be fully customized with the help of the Hyte Nexus Software. This touchscreen offers almost limitless potential, allowing you to manage system information, create shortcuts, and interact with your PC in new ways. This section will guide you through the process of installing the Hyte Nexus Software, using it for touchscreen customization, creating shortcuts and widgets, and troubleshooting any issues that might arise during the setup.

Installing Hyte Nexus Software:

Before you can begin customizing and utilizing the touchscreen, you will first need to install the Hyte Nexus Software on your PC. This software is designed to work in conjunction with the Y70's touchscreen, providing all the necessary tools to take full advantage of its features. Fortunately, installing the software is a simple and straightforward process.

1. Download the Software:

Start by downloading the Hyte Nexus Software from the official Hyte website or via the Hyte Y70 Touch's support page. Make sure you are downloading the most recent version of the software to ensure compatibility and access to the latest features.

2. Run the Installer:

Once downloaded, run the installer and follow the on-screen instructions. The installation process will automatically detect your touchscreen hardware and configure it for use. You may be prompted to restart your PC once the installation is complete.

3. Driver Installation:

During the installation process, the software will install any necessary drivers for the touchscreen to function properly.

Ensure that the drivers are correctly installed by checking the Device Manager in Windows after the installation is complete. If any issues arise, the software will likely prompt you with suggestions for troubleshooting.

4. Verify the Installation:

Once the installation is complete, launch the Hyte Nexus Software to ensure it has been correctly installed. The software interface should recognize the touchscreen immediately, and you will be prompted to begin customizing the display.

Using the Software for Touchscreen Customization:

The Hyte Nexus Software provides users with a powerful and intuitive interface to customize the 14.1-inch touchscreen to suit their specific needs. After the installation, you can begin to explore the various ways the touchscreen can be used, such as displaying system stats, running applications, or simply enhancing the overall look of your system.

1. Touchscreen Orientation and Display Settings:

The software allows you to configure the orientation and resolution of the touchscreen. By default, the screen should be set up in landscape orientation, but you can adjust the display settings within the software if you prefer to use it in portrait mode. You can also adjust the brightness and contrast to match your personal preferences or the ambient lighting in your room.

2. Customizing the Display Layout:

The main feature of the touchscreen is its ability to display various widgets, system stats, or even custom content. You can choose from a wide range of pre-configured layouts within the software or create your own. The layout editor allows you to drag and drop elements such as system temperature readings, CPU usage, GPU stats, and network information onto the touchscreen.

3. Interactive Widgets:

The Hyte Nexus Software includes a library of interactive widgets that can be added to the touchscreen, such as clock displays, weather widgets, and media controls. These widgets can be customized in size and position, allowing you to create a layout that best fits your needs.

4. Advanced Features:

The software also enables you to use the touchscreen for more advanced functions, such as controlling fan speeds, adjusting RGB lighting settings, or monitoring system performance in real-time. These features provide a deeper level of interactivity, making your Hyte Y70 Touch case not only a visually stunning enclosure but also a powerful control center for your PC.

Creating Shortcuts and Widgets:

One of the most exciting aspects of the Hyte Nexus Software is the ability to create custom shortcuts and widgets that make your touchscreen even more functional. This section will guide you through the process of setting up shortcuts and widgets to improve your workflow and enhance the overall user experience.

1. Creating Shortcuts:

Shortcuts allow you to quickly access applications or tools from your touchscreen without having to navigate through your desktop. To create a shortcut, simply open the Hyte Nexus Software and go to the Shortcut Manager. Here, you can select the application or file you want to create a shortcut for, and drag it onto the touchscreen layout. You can then resize the shortcut icon, label it, and place it wherever you like on the screen.

2. Adding Widgets:

In addition to shortcuts, widgets can be added to the touchscreen to display useful information or interactive elements. Popular widget types include system information (such as CPU, GPU, and memory usage), weather updates, calendar events, and control widgets (for managing media, system volume, and more). To add a widget, simply select the widget type from the software's widget library and drag it onto the touchscreen.

3. Customizing Widgets:

Each widget is customizable, allowing you to modify its size, position, and appearance. Some widgets can be configured to display different types of data (e.g., changing the display from

CPU usage to CPU temperature), while others offer interactive options, such as adjusting the volume or switching between applications. This level of customization gives you the flexibility to tailor the touchscreen to your unique needs.

Troubleshooting Software Issues:

As with any software, there may be occasional issues or glitches during the setup or use of the Hyte Nexus Software. While Hyte's software is generally stable and well-supported, here are some common troubleshooting steps to resolve any problems you might encounter.

1. Touchscreen Not Responding:

If the touchscreen becomes unresponsive, first check the physical connection between the touchscreen and your PC. Ensure the cables are securely connected. If everything appears to be properly connected, try restarting your PC to reset the touchscreen's drivers. You can also try recalibrating the touchscreen from within the Hyte Nexus Software to improve responsiveness.

2. Software Not Detecting the Touchscreen:

If the software doesn't detect the touchscreen after installation, ensure that you've installed the correct drivers. You can check the Device Manager to verify the touchscreen is listed under Human Interface Devices. If the drivers are missing or outdated, visit the Hyte website to download and install the latest drivers.

3. Display or Touchscreen Displaying Incorrectly:

If the display is not showing correctly or the touchscreen appears distorted, verify that the resolution settings are correctly configured within the Hyte Nexus Software. You can adjust the screen orientation and resolution settings to ensure the display is aligned properly. Additionally, updating the software to the latest version can help fix any graphical glitches.

4. Touchscreen Widgets Not Displaying Properly:

If certain widgets are not displaying correctly or are malfunctioning, try removing and re-adding them to the layout. Some widgets may also require you to restart the Hyte Nexus Software to function properly after configuration. Ensure that you have the latest version of the software installed, as updates often fix compatibility issues with certain widgets.

By following these steps, you can maximize the potential of the Hyte Y70 Touch's touchscreen, creating a highly customizable and interactive interface for your PC. With the Hyte Nexus Software, managing your system's performance, creating shortcuts, and adding widgets becomes a simple and enjoyable task. If any issues arise, the troubleshooting tips provided should help you resolve them efficiently, allowing you to enjoy all that the Hyte Y70 Touch case has to offer.

Chapter 7.

Advanced Customization

The Hyte Y70 Touch case is not only a stylish and functional case, but it also offers a high degree of customization to meet the needs of power users and PC enthusiasts. Whether you're aiming to create a visually stunning build, optimize airflow, or add additional components, the Y70 Touch provides multiple avenues for customization. This subchapter will guide you through some of the more advanced customization options available, including setting up the vertical GPU riser cable, adjusting fan and radiator configurations, installing additional PCIe expansion cards, and optimizing cable management for clean aesthetics.

Vertical GPU Riser Cable Setup:

One of the standout features of the Hyte Y70 Touch is its ability to mount the GPU vertically. Vertical GPU mounting has become increasingly popular due to the aesthetic appeal it offers, allowing the user to showcase their high-end graphics card. The Y70 Touch comes with a PCIe riser cable to facilitate this setup, but proper installation and alignment are key to ensuring a safe and functional vertical GPU configuration.

1. Installing the PCIe Riser Cable:

The first step in setting up a vertical GPU is to connect the PCIe riser cable to the motherboard's PCIe x16 slot. The riser cable is designed to allow the GPU to be mounted vertically while still providing a secure and stable connection. Carefully insert the riser cable into the motherboard's PCIe slot, ensuring that it is seated correctly. It's important to handle the riser cable gently to avoid damaging the connectors. Once the riser cable is in place, secure it to the case using the provided mounts.

2. Mounting the GPU:

After the riser cable is installed, the next step is to mount the GPU itself. Carefully insert the PCIe connector on your GPU into the riser cable's other end. Align the GPU with the vertical mount slots on the Hyte Y70 Touch case, ensuring that it is oriented correctly. Use the provided screws to secure the GPU to the case. When mounted vertically, the GPU will be on display through the case's clear side panel, giving your build a high-end, aesthetic appeal.

3. Cable Management for the GPU:

Once the GPU is installed, you'll need to ensure the riser cable is routed neatly. The Hyte Y70 Touch provides cable management options for neatly tucking away the riser cable and preventing it from obstructing airflow. Use the cable routing holes in the case to secure the cable along the back of the case, ensuring that it doesn't interfere with other components or create a cluttered look.

Adjusting Fan and Radiator Configurations:

The Hyte Y70 Touch provides ample cooling potential, allowing you to configure multiple fans and radiators to ensure optimal thermal performance. Customizing fan placement and radiator installation is a key part of building a high-performance system, especially when you're running powerful components like high-end CPUs and GPUs.

1. Fan Placement and Configurations:

The Y70 Touch allows for the installation of up to three 120mm or two 140mm fans on the front panel, two 120mm fans on the top panel, and one 120mm fan at the rear. There is no fan included in the box, so you will need to purchase fans based on your desired cooling requirements. You should begin by considering the airflow direction fans can either be configured as intake (bringing air into the case) or exhaust (pushing air out of the case).

Front Panel Fan Configuration:

If you are planning to use the front panel for intake fans, install three 120mm or two 140mm fans to bring cool air into the case. This will improve the overall airflow and ensure that your components, especially the GPU and motherboard, remain cool under load.

Top Panel Fan Configuration:

The top panel is ideal for exhaust fans since hot air naturally rises. Installing two 120mm fans here will help expel warm air from the case, preventing thermal buildup near the CPU and GPU.

Rear Panel Fan Configuration:

The rear panel can accommodate a 120mm fan, which should be used for exhaust to ensure that warm air is effectively pulled out from the case, aiding in the overall cooling performance.

2. Radiator Installation:

If you're planning to install a custom liquid cooling solution or AIO cooler, the Hyte Y70 Touch supports radiator mounts for both the front and top panels. A 240mm or 360mm radiator can be installed at the front for cooling the CPU or GPU, while a 240mm radiator can be mounted at the top for additional cooling capacity.

Front Radiator Mount:

The front of the Y70 Touch case can house a 240mm or 360mm radiator, depending on the size of the radiator and fans you choose to install. This space can support custom loops or AIO coolers, offering cooling solutions for both the CPU and GPU.

Top Radiator Mount:

The top panel can support a 240mm radiator, making it a great option for cooling your CPU or GPU. Depending on your build, this radiator can either be used as an intake or exhaust, depending on the overall airflow configuration.

Installing Additional PCIe Expansion Cards:

The Hyte Y70 Touch features multiple PCIe slots, allowing you to install a variety of expansion cards, such as sound cards, networking cards, and capture cards. While the vertical GPU mount takes up the primary PCIe x16 slot, you still have access to additional PCIe slots for installing other cards.

1. Selecting and Installing PCIe Cards:

After completing the vertical GPU setup, you can install additional PCIe cards into the available slots. These could include sound cards, Wi-Fi cards, or capture cards for streaming. Start by carefully selecting the appropriate card and aligning it with the corresponding PCIe slot on the motherboard. Gently insert the card into the slot, making sure it is properly seated. Secure the card with screws to prevent it from shifting.

2. PCIe Slot Considerations:

The Y70 Touch has several PCIe slots, but when the GPU is mounted vertically, only half-height PCIe cards can be installed in the remaining slots. This limitation may restrict the types of expansion cards you can use, but fortunately, there are several half-height options available, such as smaller networking cards or sound cards, which should fit within the available space.

Optimizing Cable Management for Clean Aesthetics:

One of the hallmarks of a well-built PC is cable management. The Hyte Y70 Touch offers plenty of options for hiding cables and ensuring a clean and organized interior. Proper cable management not only improves the aesthetics of your build but also enhances airflow by reducing cable clutter.

1. Cable Routing:

The Y70 Touch case features multiple cable routing channels along the backside of the case, allowing you to neatly route cables out of sight. Use these channels to run cables from the power supply unit (PSU), motherboard, fans, and other components. Secure the cables using zip ties or Velcro straps to prevent them from obstructing airflow or becoming tangled.

2. Cable Trays and Cable Pass-Throughs:

The case includes several cable pass-throughs that allow you to route cables neatly behind the motherboard tray. These pass-throughs help maintain a clean interior while also providing the necessary space to manage the cables. The cable tray located behind the PSU is a great place to hide cables from the power supply, ensuring that they do not obstruct the rest of the build.

3. Maintaining Aesthetic Balance:

A clean interior can dramatically improve the overall aesthetics of your build, especially when you have a vertical GPU on display. Keep cables organized and hidden to avoid detracting from the visual appeal of your components. Pay attention to fan cables, RGB lighting, and other peripherals to ensure they are routed neatly without interfering with airflow or the overall design of the build.

By focusing on advanced customization options such as vertical GPU setup, fan and radiator configurations, additional PCIe card installations, and cable management, the Hyte Y70 Touch allows users to create a truly unique and optimized PC build. Whether you prioritize aesthetics, airflow, or functionality, this case provides the flexibility and tools needed to bring your vision to life.

Chapter 8.

Maintenance and Care

Maintaining the Hyte Y70 Touch is essential to ensuring that your build remains in top condition, both in terms of aesthetics and functionality. Like any high-performance PC case, the Y70 Touch requires regular cleaning, proper maintenance of the touchscreen, dust management, and monitoring of internal temperatures to ensure that all components continue to perform optimally. In this subchapter, we will explore how to care for your Y70 Touch case, covering cleaning procedures, touchscreen maintenance, airflow management, and checking internal temperatures.

Cleaning the Hyte Y70 Touch Case:

Over time, dust and debris will accumulate in your Hyte Y70 Touch case, which can negatively affect both the aesthetics and the performance of your build. Regular cleaning is essential to maintain the case's sleek look and to prevent dust from obstructing airflow. Cleaning the case is a straightforward process, but it's important to follow the correct steps to avoid damaging components.

1. External Cleaning:

Start by turning off your PC, disconnecting all power sources, and opening the case. The Y70 Touch has a tempered glass side panel, which should be cleaned gently to avoid scratches. Use a microfiber cloth to wipe down the glass, ensuring a streak-free finish. If the exterior is particularly dirty, you can dampen the microfiber cloth with water or a mild cleaning solution. Avoid harsh chemicals, as they can damage the case's finish.

For the aluminum panels on the front, top, and bottom of the case, a microfiber cloth or soft brush should be sufficient for removing dust and dirt. If you prefer, you can use a can of compressed air to blow away dust from crevices that may be harder to reach.

2. Interior Cleaning:

Once the exterior is cleaned, it's time to focus on the interior of the case. Use a soft brush to gently remove dust from sensitive areas such as the motherboard, GPU, storage devices, and power supply unit (PSU). If you have installed liquid cooling systems, be cautious around the tubing and radiator fins. A can of compressed air is ideal for blowing out dust from tight spots without causing any physical damage to components. When using compressed air, hold the can upright and spray short bursts to avoid moisture buildup inside the case.

Regularly cleaning the interior of your case ensures that dust does not accumulate on vital components, which could negatively impact system performance.

Maintaining the Touchscreen:

The 14.1-inch 4K touchscreen is one of the Hyte Y70 Touch case's standout features, but like any display, it requires proper maintenance to keep it functioning at its best. While the screen itself is durable, care should be taken to avoid scratches and smudges that could interfere with the display quality.

1. Cleaning the Touchscreen:

The touchscreen can attract dust, fingerprints, and smudges, especially if you use it frequently. To clean the screen, use a microfiber cloth that is soft and lint-free. Gently wipe the screen in a circular motion to remove fingerprints and other marks. If necessary, slightly dampen the cloth with water or a mild screen cleaner. Avoid using harsh chemicals or abrasive materials, as these could scratch or damage the touchscreen surface.

2. Touchscreen Calibration and Software Maintenance:

If you notice any issues with touchscreen responsiveness or functionality, it may be time to recalibrate the display. In most cases, Hyte's Nexus software allows you to reset or recalibrate the touchscreen for optimal performance. Additionally, ensure that you are running the latest version of the software, as updates may include important fixes or new features. Always check for software updates regularly to ensure that the touchscreen and case software continue to function smoothly.

Ensuring Proper Airflow and Dust Management:

One of the most critical aspects of maintaining a high-performance PC build is ensuring that the system has proper airflow. Without efficient airflow, components such as the CPU, GPU, and power supply can overheat, leading to performance throttling or even hardware damage. The Hyte Y70 Touch case is designed with airflow in mind, but it's still important to regularly check and maintain airflow to keep your build running smoothly.

1. Airflow Design:

The Y70 Touch offers several fan mounting points that allow you to configure the airflow system for optimal cooling. Proper airflow involves a balanced intake and exhaust configuration. The front panel should generally be configured for intake fans, while the top and rear should be used for exhaust to expel hot air from the case. Check that all installed fans are working properly, and ensure that they are configured correctly to maintain consistent airflow.

2. Dust Filters:

The Y70 Touch comes equipped with dust filters on the front, top, and bottom panels. These filters help trap dust before it enters the case, reducing the amount of dust that settles on your components. However, dust filters can become clogged over time and need to be cleaned regularly. To clean the filters, simply remove them from the case and use a soft brush or compressed air to blow away any accumulated dust. For stubborn dirt, you can wash the filters with water and mild soap, then allow them to dry completely before reinstalling them.

3. Preventing Dust Build-Up:

While dust filters are essential, they are not foolproof. To further reduce dust accumulation inside your case, avoid placing your PC in dusty environments. Regularly cleaning the external case and fans, and ensuring that your room has proper ventilation, will also help minimize the amount of dust entering the system.

Checking Internal Temperatures:

One of the most important aspects of maintaining your Hyte Y70 Touch is ensuring that your system's internal temperatures remain within safe limits. Excessive heat can reduce the lifespan of components and lead to system instability. Regularly checking the internal temperatures of key components such as the CPU, GPU, and motherboard is crucial to keeping your system running smoothly.

1. Monitoring Temperatures:

Use software tools like HWMonitor, CoreTemp, or MSI Afterburner to monitor the temperatures of your system's components. Most modern motherboards also come with software that allows you to check the internal temperatures. For optimal performance, the CPU should ideally remain below 80°C under load, while the GPU should stay below 85°C. If your temperatures are consistently higher than these thresholds, you may need to adjust your cooling configuration or check for airflow issues.

2. Improving Cooling:

If you notice that your temperatures are higher than desired, it may be time to adjust your fan speeds, reinstall thermal paste on the CPU, or clean the fans and heatsinks to ensure proper heat dissipation. You can also consider adding more fans or improving the configuration of your existing cooling system to ensure that hot air is being properly expelled from the case.

3. Proactive Maintenance:

Preventative maintenance is key to ensuring that your system remains stable and cool over time. Regularly cleaning your case, checking fan performance, and monitoring temperatures will help you spot potential issues before they escalate. If you notice that temperatures are steadily increasing despite proper maintenance, it may be time to upgrade your cooling system or reapply thermal paste to key components.

Conclusion:

Maintaining your Hyte Y70 Touch case is an essential part of ensuring that your system performs optimally over time. Regular cleaning, proper maintenance of the touchscreen, managing airflow and dust, and monitoring internal temperatures will not only help keep your build looking great but also ensure that it runs smoothly and efficiently. By following these maintenance practices, you can maximize the lifespan of your components and ensure that your system continues to perform at its best.

Chapter 9.

Troubleshooting

Building a PC with the Hyte Y70 Touch case can be an exciting experience, but like any complex hardware setup, it is possible to encounter a few bumps along the way. Whether you're dealing with installation issues, touchscreen malfunctions, software bugs, or cooling problems, troubleshooting is a necessary skill to ensure your system runs smoothly. This subchapter will guide you through some common troubleshooting steps for the Y70 Touch, addressing installation problems, touchscreen issues, software bugs, cooling concerns, and the challenges that come with vertical GPU installation.

Common Installation Issues:

During the installation of components in the Hyte Y70 Touch, users may experience issues that prevent them from completing the build. These problems typically arise from hardware compatibility, space constraints, or improper assembly. Here are a few common issues and their solutions:

1. Component Fit Issues:

The Y70 Touch is a spacious case, but large components like high-end GPUs and large motherboards may present some fitting challenges. The vertical GPU mounting can limit available space for other expansion cards, and there might be instances where you need to adjust the placement of cables or parts. Ensure that your motherboard and GPU dimensions are compatible with the case by referring to the manufacturer's specifications. If necessary, adjust cable management and reposition other components to allow for more space.

2. Cable Management Problems:

Proper cable management is essential not just for aesthetics but also for airflow. Sometimes cables may obstruct airflow or interfere with component installation. To avoid this, use the cable management channels, tie-down points, and Velcro straps provided in the case to secure cables neatly. If cables are too long, consider using cable extensions or shorter cables that better fit the case's layout. If you still face issues, consider investing in a modular PSU to reduce excess cables that can clutter the interior.

3. Mounting Hardware:

Missing or incorrect mounting hardware is a common installation issue. Double-check that the screws, standoffs, and brackets provided in the box match the components you're installing. If you're missing parts or have incompatible screws, it's important to reach out to Hyte customer support for replacements.

Touchscreen Not Working:

The 14.1-inch touchscreen is one of the standout features of the Hyte Y70 Touch, but users sometimes experience issues with it not functioning properly. Here are the main troubleshooting steps if the touchscreen is not working:

1. Check Connections:

If the touchscreen is unresponsive, start by checking all connections. Ensure that the DisplayPort and power cables are properly connected to both the touchscreen and the motherboard or power supply. A loose connection could prevent the screen from powering up.

2. Display Driver Issues:

The touchscreen's display may not function properly if the necessary drivers are not installed. Ensure that you have installed Hyte's Nexus software, which includes the required drivers for the touchscreen. You can find the latest software version on Hyte's official website. If you suspect that the driver installation is faulty, uninstall and reinstall the software.

3. Power Supply Issues:

If the touchscreen is not powering on, it could be due to an issue with the power supply. Ensure that the PSU provides adequate power for all components, including the touchscreen. If you have recently installed a new PSU or upgraded your system, verify that the power output meets the requirements for the Y70 Touch.

4. Reboot and Reset:

A simple reboot or reset of the system can sometimes resolve touchscreen issues. If the touchscreen still doesn't respond, try disconnecting it, waiting a few moments, and reconnecting it. Some users have found that rebooting with the touchscreen unplugged and then reconnecting it works.

Software Bugs and Fixes:

Since the Hyte Y70 Touch case relies on the Nexus software for touchscreen functionality and other customization features, users may encounter bugs or glitches that hinder optimal performance. Here's how to handle software-related issues:

1. Check for Updates:

If you're experiencing software-related issues, the first thing to do is check for updates to the Hyte Nexus software. Hyte regularly releases updates to fix bugs and improve functionality. Visit the official website or use the built-in update feature in the Nexus software to download the latest version.

2. Software Reinstallation:

If the software is malfunctioning, it may be helpful to reinstall it. Uninstall the Nexus software from your system and then download the latest version from Hyte's website. Reinstall the software and check if the issue is resolved.

3. Configuration Conflicts:

Sometimes, software bugs can occur due to conflicting settings or profiles. If you have multiple profiles set up in the Nexus software, try switching to a default profile to see if the issue persists. Resetting the software to default settings can often clear up issues caused by conflicting customizations.

4. Contacting Support:

If the software continues to malfunction despite troubleshooting, you may need to contact Hyte's customer support. They can provide advanced troubleshooting tips, including specific fixes for known issues or compatibility problems.

Resolving Cooling Issues:

Efficient cooling is vital for maintaining your PC's performance and longevity. If you encounter cooling problems such as high temperatures or noisy fans, follow these steps to resolve the issue:

1. Check Fan and Radiator Placement:

Ensure that your fans are correctly mounted and oriented for proper airflow. Fans should be placed so that they intake cool air from the front and expel hot air from the rear or top. Verify that there are no obstructions blocking the airflow, such as cables or incorrectly positioned components. If necessary, adjust the fan positions for optimal airflow.

2. Fan and Radiator Installation:

If your system is running hot despite having fans, check whether the radiators and AIO coolers are installed correctly. Radiators should be mounted in positions where they can efficiently expel heat. Ensure that the pump and fans are connected to the correct headers on the motherboard or fan controller. You may also want to increase the fan speed using the motherboard's fan control software or BIOS settings to ensure adequate cooling during intense workloads.

3. Reapply Thermal Paste:

If the CPU or GPU temperatures are higher than expected, it may be time to reapply thermal paste. Over time, thermal paste can degrade and lose its effectiveness. Remove the old paste carefully, clean the surface, and apply a fresh layer of thermal paste to ensure efficient heat transfer from the processor to the cooler.

4. Monitor Temperatures:

Use hardware monitoring software to track the internal temperatures of your system. Tools like HWMonitor, MSI Afterburner, or CoreTemp will allow you to monitor the temperatures of your CPU, GPU, and other components in real-time. If temperatures are too high, further adjustments to the cooling system may be necessary.

Accessing the Motherboard with Vertical GPU Installation:

Installing the GPU in the vertical mount position can present challenges when accessing the motherboard for tasks such as adding memory, connecting cables, or upgrading components. Here are a few troubleshooting tips for working with a vertical GPU mount:

1. Move GPU Temporarily:

If you need to access the motherboard for any reason, such as installing RAM or connecting cables, consider temporarily removing the GPU from the vertical mount. This will give you more room to work with and prevent potential damage to the GPU or other components.

2. Use Flexible Tools:

In some cases, vertical GPUs can obstruct direct access to certain areas of the motherboard. Consider using flexible tools, such as long screwdrivers or angled tweezers, to reach tight spaces and avoid removing the GPU every time you need to perform maintenance.

3. Install Low-Profile Expansion Cards:

When using a vertical GPU mount, it's important to remember that other expansion cards will need to be half-height. Make sure you choose low-profile cards for components such as sound cards or capture cards to avoid conflicts with the GPU and to ensure that everything fits inside the case.

By following these troubleshooting tips, you can address common issues with the Hyte Y70 Touch case and ensure that your system continues to perform at its best. Remember, troubleshooting is a normal part of the PC-building process, and with patience and attention to detail, most issues can be resolved quickly.

Chapter 10.

Specifications

The Hyte Y70 Touch is a unique and feature-packed PC case designed for users who prioritize aesthetics, functionality, and cutting-edge technology. With its standout feature of a 14.1-inch touchscreen, the Y70 Touch offers a combination of advanced components and compatibility options to meet the demands of high-end PC builds. This chapter dives into the full technical specifications of the case, detailing the dimensions, supported components, and configuration options available to users. Additionally, we'll explore the compatibility of key components, such as motherboards, GPUs, PSUs, and more, ensuring that you can make the best choice when building your system within this impressive chassis.

Full Technical Specifications of the Hyte Y70 Touch:

The Hyte Y70 Touch case boasts a sleek and modern design, offering ample space for high-performance components. Its full specifications provide an understanding of its capabilities, size, and the features it incorporates for an optimal user experience. Here are the key technical specifications of the case:

1. Overall Dimensions:

Height:

510 mm (20.08 inches)

Width:

240 mm (9.45 inches)

Depth:

490 mm (19.29 inches)

Weight:

11.6 kg (25.57 lbs)

The Y70 Touch is a substantial case that can accommodate large components and provide plenty of space for cable management, custom cooling setups, and expansion cards.

2. Material and Build:

Material:

Tempered glass (front, side, and rear panels) and steel frame

Finish:

Matte black or white powder-coated finish

The steel frame provides durability and structural integrity, while the tempered glass panels offer a clear view of the internal components, enhancing the overall aesthetics of the build.

3. Front I/O Ports:

USB 3.0 Ports:

2 x Type-A

USB 3.1 Gen 2 Port:

1 x Type-C

Audio Ports:

1 x 3.5mm headphone, 1 x 3.5mm microphone

Power Button:

1 x Power button

Reset Button:

1 x Reset button

RGB Controls:

1 x RGB control button (if applicable)

The I/O panel is placed at the top of the case, allowing easy access to commonly used ports and controls.

4. Compatibility:

Motherboards:

ATX, Micro ATX, Mini ITX

Expansion Slots:

7 PCIe expansion slots

GPU Compatibility:

Supports vertical GPU mount, accommodates GPUs up to 355 mm (13.98 inches) in length

CPU Cooler Height:

Supports air coolers up to 170 mm (6.69 inches) tall

Radiator Compatibility:

Front, top, and bottom radiator mounting options, supports up to a 360 mm radiator (front), 240 mm radiator (top), and 120 mm radiator (bottom).

This extensive compatibility range ensures the Y70 Touch can support a wide variety of high-performance components, from large GPUs to advanced cooling solutions.

5. 14.1-inch Touchscreen:

Resolution:

1100 x 3840 pixels

Aspect Ratio:

16:9

Panel Type:

IPS LCD, capacitive touch

Functionality:

Used for system monitoring, shortcuts, widget customization, and even acting as a second screen for different applications

Connectivity:

DisplayPort for video, USB for touch functionality, and 12V for power

The touchscreen is the signature feature of the Y70 Touch case, offering a customizable interface that can display system information, widgets, or serve as a secondary display for apps. This large, high-resolution display adds a touch of luxury and futuristic flair to your build.

6. Fan and Cooling Options:

Included Fans:

None (fans are not included, but the case supports custom fan installation)

Supported Fan Sizes:

Front:

3 x 120mm or 2 x 140mm

Top:

3 x 120mm or 2 x 140mm

Bottom:

1 x 120mm

Rear:

1 x 120mm

Fan Mounting:

The case supports multiple mounting points for optimal airflow, ensuring users can configure the system to match their cooling requirements.

Radiator Compatibility:

Supports up to a 360mm radiator in the front, 240mm radiator at the top, and a 120mm radiator at the bottom for users looking to build custom water-cooling loops or install an AIO cooler.

7. Storage Support:

2.5-inch SSD Slots:

2 x 2.5-inch

3.5-inch HDD Slots:

2 x 3.5-inch

Additional Storage:

2 x 2.5-inch SSD mounting points can be added with optional brackets for further expansion.

The Y70 Touch case offers flexible storage options, allowing users to install both SSDs and HDDs in a variety of configurations. The additional space for SSDs ensures that you can have high-speed storage alongside traditional mass storage drives.

8. Cable Management:

The Y70 Touch features extensive cable management options with multiple cable tie-down points, rubber grommets for cable passes, and ample space behind the motherboard tray for routing cables neatly. These features are designed to help you achieve a clean build while maintaining optimal airflow and aesthetics.

Component Compatibility:

The Hyte Y70 Touch is designed to accommodate a wide variety of high-performance components, ensuring that users can build systems tailored to their needs. Here's a closer look at the key components that are compatible with this case:

1. Motherboard Compatibility:

The Y70 Touch supports a range of motherboard sizes, including ATX, Micro ATX, and Mini ITX. This compatibility ensures that users can select from a wide array of motherboards, whether they're looking for a standard ATX board with plenty of expansion slots or a smaller Mini ITX motherboard for a more compact build. The case's flexible mounting options make it easy to install these motherboards securely.

2. GPU Compatibility:

One of the standout features of the Y70 Touch is its ability to accommodate large graphics cards. With a vertical GPU mount, it can fit GPUs up to 355 mm (13.98 inches) in length, which includes most of the current high-end GPUs on the market, including models from NVIDIA and AMD. The vertical GPU mount not only ensures sufficient space for large cards but also provides a unique and eye-catching aesthetic for your build. The case also includes a custom PCIe riser cable for proper vertical installation.

3. PSU Compatibility:

The case supports standard ATX PSUs up to 200 mm (7.87 inches) in length, providing ample space for even high-wattage power supplies. The PSU compartment is well-separated from the rest of the build, ensuring proper airflow and cable management. The spacious PSU bay allows for easy installation and maintenance of your power supply unit, making it suitable for both modular and non-modular PSUs.

4. Cooling Compatibility:

The Y70 Touch is highly compatible with custom cooling solutions. It can support multiple radiators, including a 360mm radiator in the front and 240mm radiators at the top and bottom, giving users flexibility in designing their cooling loops. This case can accommodate both air cooling and liquid cooling solutions, making it suitable for a wide range of setups.

5. Storage Compatibility:

The case supports both SSD and HDD installations, allowing users to build their system with ample storage capacity. It offers two 3.5-inch HDD slots and two 2.5-inch SSD slots for solid-state and traditional hard drives, ensuring users can choose the right combination of performance and capacity. The option to add additional SSD mounts further enhances the case's storage capabilities.

Conclusion:

The Hyte Y70 Touch is a versatile and spacious PC case with impressive specifications that support a wide range of components. With its ability to accommodate large GPUs, multiple storage devices, and advanced cooling solutions, the Y70 Touch provides the flexibility needed for high-end builds. The integration of a 14.1-inch touchscreen adds a unique and customizable feature, setting this case apart from others on the market. Whether you're building a gaming rig, a workstation, or a custom water-cooled system, the Y70 Touch offers the compatibility and features necessary to make your build a success.

Chapter 11.

Warranty and Support

When purchasing a premium product like the Hyte Y70 Touch, it is essential to understand the warranty and support services provided by the manufacturer. A comprehensive warranty ensures that you are covered in the event of defects or other issues, while responsive customer support helps address concerns and troubleshoot problems. In this chapter, we will outline the warranty information, provide guidance on contacting Hyte support, and offer solutions to frequently asked questions (FAQs) to ensure you have all the information you need for a smooth experience with your Hyte Y70 Touch case.

Warranty Information:

Hyte offers a standard warranty on all of its products, including the Y70 Touch. This warranty provides protection against defects in materials and workmanship, ensuring that users can have peace of mind when purchasing their products.

1. Length of Warranty:

The standard warranty for the Hyte Y70 Touch case is two years from the date of purchase. This warranty covers any defects or issues that arise from normal use and is valid for both the case itself and the included components, such as the touchscreen and PCIe riser cable. The warranty period starts from the date you purchase the product, and you will need to keep your receipt or proof of purchase to claim warranty services.

2. Coverage:

The warranty covers:

Manufacturing defects in the case structure, including the frame and panels.

Defects in the touchscreen, including failure of the capacitive touch functionality or screen issues caused by manufacturing faults.

Defective components, such as the PCIe riser cable that is part of the case.

Failure of internal wiring or other integral parts directly related to the case's assembly.

However, the warranty does not cover issues caused by:

Improper handling or misuse of the product.

Physical damage (e.g., cracked glass, scratched panels).

Modification or customization that alters the original design of the case (e.g., removing panels, installing non-approved components).

Damage caused by external factors, such as power surges, fire, or water exposure.

3. How to Claim Warranty:

If you encounter any issues covered under the warranty, Hyte provides a straightforward process to claim warranty service. The first step is to contact Hyte's customer service team, where you'll need to provide:

Proof of purchase (receipt or invoice).

A description of the issue.

Photos or videos of the defect, if applicable.

Your contact information and shipping address.

Once Hyte's support team receives your claim, they will assess the situation and guide you through the next steps, which may include sending the product back for repair, replacement, or refund.

Contacting Hyte Support:

For any questions, concerns, or warranty claims, contacting Hyte's customer support team is your best route. Here's how to get in touch with them for assistance:

1. Customer Support Portal:

Hyte provides an online support portal where users can submit tickets for various issues. The portal allows for easy tracking of your inquiries and ensures that your support request is routed to the appropriate department. To submit a support ticket, follow these steps:

Visit the Hyte support website.

Sign in to your account or create one.

Navigate to the support section and select the relevant issue (e.g., warranty claim, technical support, product inquiry).

Provide detailed information about the issue, including any supporting documentation or media (photos/videos).

Submit the ticket, and you will receive a response within 1-2 business days.

2. Email Support:

Alternatively, you can reach out to Hyte's customer support team via email. The support email is typically listed on the official Hyte website under the contact section. Ensure that your email includes:

A brief description of your issue.

Your purchase details (receipt or order number).

Any supporting images or documentation of the problem.

3. Phone Support:

For more urgent inquiries or for those who prefer speaking directly with a support representative, Hyte offers phone support during business hours. The phone number for customer service can be found on the contact page of their website. It's helpful to have your purchase details and a clear description of the issue on hand when calling.

4. Social Media:

Hyte is also active on social media platforms, including Facebook, Twitter, and Instagram. While social media channels are primarily used for product updates, promotions, and community engagement, you can also direct support inquiries through direct messages. This can be a convenient way to get an initial response or to inquire about ongoing support tickets.

FAQs (Frequently Asked Questions):

The following is a compilation of common questions that users may have regarding the Hyte Y70 Touch case, along with their answers. These FAQs can help clarify some of the most frequently encountered issues or concerns.

1. Do I need to buy fans separately for the Y70 Touch?

Yes, the Y70 Touch case does not come with fans included. Hyte has left it up to the user to choose their preferred fan setup based on cooling needs. The case supports a wide range of fan configurations, with space for up to three 120mm fans in the front and two 140mm fans at the top, as well as other configurations for radiators and additional cooling solutions.

2. Can I use an ATX motherboard in the Y70 Touch?

Yes, the Hyte Y70 Touch supports ATX, Micro ATX, and Mini ITX motherboards. It is compatible with a variety of motherboard sizes, giving you flexibility when selecting components for your build.

3. What is the maximum GPU length supported in the Y70 Touch?

The case can accommodate GPUs up to 355 mm (13.98 inches) in length, making it compatible with most high-end GPUs, including those from NVIDIA and AMD.

4. Can I install an AIO liquid cooler in the Y70 Touch?

Yes, the Y70 Touch supports AIO liquid cooling systems. The case offers space for up to a 360mm radiator in the front and a 240mm radiator at the top, providing ample room for efficient liquid cooling setups.

5. How do I customize the touchscreen on the Y70 Touch?

To customize the touchscreen, you will need to install the Hyte Nexus Software. This software allows you to configure widgets, shortcuts, and system monitoring features. You can create personalized displays for system information, media controls, or even use the touchscreen as a second monitor for productivity.

6. What should I do if the touchscreen is not working?

If the touchscreen isn't functioning properly, make sure the DisplayPort and USB cables are securely connected to your system. You can also try reinstalling the touchscreen drivers or updating the Hyte Nexus Software. If the issue persists, contact Hyte support for further assistance.

7. Can I install a vertical GPU mount with other PCIe expansion cards?

The vertical GPU mount in the Y70 Touch uses PCIe slots, but it does limit the use of other expansion cards. Due to the space required for the vertical mount, users may need to use half-height PCIe cards for other expansions, such as sound cards or capture cards.

8. What is the maximum CPU cooler height supported in the Y70 Touch?

The Y70 Touch can support air coolers up to 170mm (6.69 inches) in height, giving you plenty of options for high-performance air cooling.

Conclusion:

The warranty and support for the Hyte Y70 Touch ensure that customers have a positive and secure ownership experience. With a clear and straightforward warranty policy, a responsive customer support team, and a robust FAQ section, users can confidently reach out for assistance when needed. The Hyte Y70 Touch is designed to offer flexibility, customization, and high-quality performance, and Hyte stands behind its products with reliable support and service to keep your system running smoothly.

Conclusion

The Hyte Y70 Touch case represents a bold step forward in PC case design, bringing together aesthetics, functionality, and cutting-edge technology in a way that's rarely seen in today's PC building market. With a unique combination of a stunning vertical GPU mount, an innovative 14.1-inch touchscreen, and impressive expansion capabilities, this case is clearly designed for those who want both performance and visual impact in their build. In this conclusion, we will take a deeper look at the final thoughts on the Hyte Y70 Touch case, summarize the key features and benefits, and assess its overall value.

Final Thoughts on the Hyte Y70 Touch Case:

The Hyte Y70 Touch is a case that immediately stands out from the crowd. From its clean, modern design to the innovative addition of a touchscreen, it's clear that Hyte is aiming for a high-end, enthusiast-focused market. The Y70 Touch offers ample space for larger components and provides significant flexibility in terms of cooling and component installation. Whether you're planning a custom liquid-cooling setup or just need a powerful and spacious case for air cooling, the Y70 Touch offers the room and design to accommodate it.

The case's standout feature is undoubtedly its 14.1-inch touchscreen. While touchscreen integration in PC cases is still a relatively new concept, Hyte's decision to include a screen that functions not just as a static display but as an interactive hub is a revolutionary step in case design. The ability to integrate custom widgets, system monitoring tools, shortcuts, and even media control into the display opens up vast possibilities for personalization. This feature will likely appeal to a wide range of users—from gamers and streamers who want to display their Twitch chat, to professionals who could use the screen for productivity tools, to enthusiasts who simply want to add a unique touch to their builds.

Despite its impressive features, the Y70 Touch does have some limitations. The vertical GPU mount, while aesthetically pleasing, restricts other PCIe expansion cards to half-height slots. This could pose an issue for users who wish to include additional components like sound cards, capture cards, or networking cards. However, for those who prioritize GPU performance and the overall visual appeal of their build, this compromise may be worth it.

Another consideration is the lack of included fans. While this allows for complete customization of the cooling solution, it also means that users will need to factor in the cost of fans or radiators when budgeting for their build. Depending on the cooling requirements of the components selected, this could add extra cost to the overall build. Additionally, the cooling performance is entirely dependent on the user's decisions regarding airflow and fan placement, meaning users must put some thought into creating an optimal configuration.

The case's build quality is top-notch, with a robust frame, sleek panels, and well-thought-out design features that provide both aesthetic appeal and functional benefits. Cable management options are plentiful, helping keep the inside of the case clean and organized, even when running a high-end configuration. The ample space inside the Y70 Touch allows users to easily accommodate large components, such as high-end GPUs, motherboards, and AIO cooling setups, making it ideal for enthusiasts building powerful systems.

Overall, the Y70 Touch is a case designed for enthusiasts, gamers, and content creators who value aesthetics, performance, and customization. It is a case that feels tailored to a specific demographic—those who want to push the boundaries of traditional PC builds and aren't afraid to invest in unique features that enhance both form and function.

Summary of Key Features and Benefits:

1. Innovative 14.1-inch Touchscreen:

The touchscreen is undoubtedly the key selling point of the Y70 Touch. This high-resolution 14.1-inch display offers immense customization potential. From viewing system stats and Twitch chat to setting up shortcuts for frequently used apps or functions, the touchscreen allows for seamless interaction with your system. It's perfect for those looking to personalize their setup and incorporate modern technology into their case design.

2. Ample Space and Versatility:

The Y70 Touch provides exceptional room for components, easily accommodating ATX, Micro ATX, and Mini ITX motherboards. The case supports large GPUs, including models like the RTX 4090, and offers up to 355mm of GPU clearance. This ample space allows for flexibility when building, whether you want to include a large liquid-cooling setup or install extra storage drives.

3. Vertical GPU Mount:

The vertical GPU mounting is a striking feature of the Y70 Touch. By showcasing the GPU in an upright position, the case adds a visual focal point that enhances the overall aesthetics of the system. Although the vertical mount limits

PCIe slots to half-height cards, this design is aimed at users who prioritize GPU visibility and are willing to compromise on additional expansion cards.

4. Premium Build Quality:

The build quality of the Y70 Touch is exceptional. Hyte has designed this case with high-end materials that not only provide durability but also offer a premium aesthetic. The tempered glass panels provide a clear view of the internals, showcasing your components and any custom cooling systems you've installed.

5. Cable Management Options:

The case comes with a plethora of cable management options, allowing users to keep their builds clean and organized. From cable tie-downs to hidden channels, the Y70 Touch provides multiple ways to route cables efficiently, which not only improves airflow but also ensures a neat and polished look.

6. Custom Cooling Configurations:

The Y70 Touch offers extensive cooling support, with mounts for up to three 120mm front fans and two 140mm top fans. Additionally, the case supports radiators up to 360mm in the front and 240mm at the top, making it an excellent choice for custom liquid-cooling setups. Users have the flexibility to optimize airflow for their specific needs, whether it's maximizing performance or minimizing noise.

7. Enhanced Functionality with Hyte Nexus Software:

The Hyte Nexus Software is a critical component of the touchscreen's functionality. It allows users to customize widgets, monitor system performance, and control various aspects of the case's touchscreen interface. The software is intuitive, user-friendly, and constantly being improved, ensuring that the touchscreen remains a valuable tool for users.

8. Premium Price for Premium Features:

The Y70 Touch comes with a premium price tag—£349.99. While this may be considered high for a case, the price reflects the advanced features and premium design. The included PCIe riser card, the touchscreen, and the robust build quality all contribute to the value of the case. However, it's important to note that the case ships fanless, so users will need to budget for their cooling solutions.

9. Target Audience:

The Hyte Y70 Touch is ideal for users who are willing to invest in a high-quality, customizable PC case. It is not a case aimed at budget-conscious builders but rather those looking to create a powerful and visually striking system. Whether you're a gamer, streamer, or content creator, this case will meet your needs, provided you're prepared for the added investment in cooling and fans.

Conclusion: A Case for the Future:

In conclusion, the Hyte Y70 Touch is a standout PC case that combines modern design with innovative technology. Its 14.1-inch touchscreen, along with exceptional expandability and cooling options, make it an appealing choice for enthusiasts looking for a premium, customizable, and visually striking case. While it may not be suitable for everyone due to its price point and the compromises made with the vertical GPU mount, it offers a level of innovation and flexibility that few other cases can match. The Y70 Touch is more than just a case it's a platform for building a truly unique and high-performance PC.

www.ingramcontent.com/pod-product-compliance
Lightning Source LLC
Chambersburg PA
CBHW071035240526
45469CB00006BD/2215